BUDDHA SHAKYAMUNI

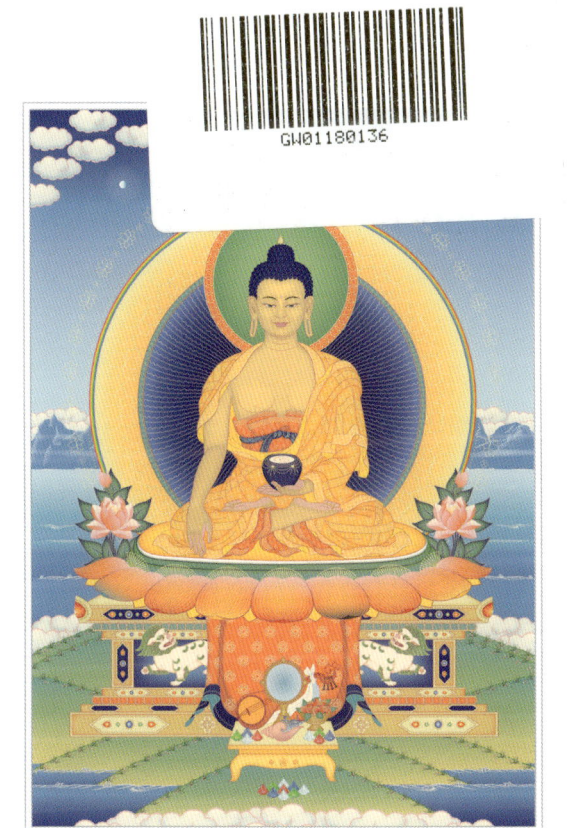

Buddha Shakyamuni is the founder of Buddhism in this world age, and the principal object of refuge for all Buddhists.

Buddha Vajradhara

*The founder and principal
Buddha of the Tantric teachings.*

The Vows and Commitments of Kadampa Buddhism

Tharpa Publications

Contents

Introduction 7

The Benefits of Going for Refuge 11

The Refuge Vows 12

The Lay Pratimoksha Vows 13

The Benefits of Bodhichitta 13

The Precepts of Aspiring Bodhichitta 14

The Root Downfalls of the Bodhisattva Vows 15

The Secondary Downfalls of the Bodhisattva Vows ... 16

The Commitments of Training the Mind 20

The Precepts of Training the Mind 21

The Nineteen Commitments of the Five
 Buddha Families 22

The Fourteen Root Downfalls of the
 Secret Mantra Vows 24

The Branch Commitments 25

The Gross Downfalls of the Secret Mantra Vows 26

The Uncommon Commitments of Mother Tantra 27

Dedication 28

Introduction

The vows and commitments of Kadampa Buddhism are guidelines for living a peaceful and compassionate way of life. They are methods to solve our own and others' problems and to make ourself and others happy. Through keeping these vows and commitments purely we avoid all negative actions, the cause of suffering for ourself and others. Ultimately they are methods for attaining the happiness of full enlightenment. For this reason we should never think that our vows and commitments are a heavy burden, but think that they have been given to us by Buddha as a way of fulfilling all our wishes.

There are three types of vows and commitments: the Pratimoksha vows, which are motivated by renunciation, the wish to attain freedom from suffering; the Bodhisattva vows, which are motivated by bodhichitta, the wish to attain enlightenment for the welfare and happiness of others; and the Tantric vows, which are motivated by the wish to attain enlightenment as quickly as possible for the benefit of others.

By taking vows all our actions become more powerful in causing happiness and in our attaining full enlightenment. If we take Bodhisattva vows our actions are more powerful than if we take only the Pratimoksha vows; and if we take the Tantric vows our actions are more powerful than if we take only the Bodhisattva vows.

There are four main causes of the degeneration of the Pratimoksha, Bodhisattva or Tantric vows, which are known as the 'four doors of receiving downfalls'. These are: not knowing what the downfalls are, lack of respect for Buddha's instructions, strong delusions and non-conscientiousness.

To close the first door, we should learn what the downfalls are and how they are incurred. We can do this by listening to teachings on the subject or by reading authentic commentaries.

To close the second door, we should try to overcome disrespect by contemplating the following:

Since Buddha is omniscient, knowing all past, present and future phenomena simultaneously and directly, and since he has great compassion for all living beings without exception, there is no valid reason for developing disrespect towards his teachings. It is only due to ignorance that I sometimes disbelieve them.

To close the third door, we should try to subdue our strong delusions by practising the meditations described in *The New Meditation Handbook*. If, by practising the stages of the path to enlightenment, Lamrim, we are able always to maintain good intentions such as love, compassion and bodhichitta, there will be no basis for incurring Pratimoksha or Bodhisattva downfalls; and if, by practising the generation and completion stages of Highest Yoga Tantra, we overcome ordinary appearances and ordinary conceptions, there will be no basis for incurring Tantric downfalls.

We can close the fourth door, non-conscientiousness, by repeatedly bringing to mind the disadvantages of incurring downfalls and the advantages of pure moral discipline. In this way, we become more conscientious.

In brief, the method for preventing our vows from degenerating is to train in renunciation, bodhichitta, the correct view of emptiness, generation stage and completion stage. By sincerely practising these, we overcome our ordinary attitudes and control our mind, thereby removing any basis for downfalls.

Suggested reading: *The Bodhisattva Vow, How to Understand the Mind, Meaningful to Behold* and *A Handbook for the Daily Practice of Bodhisattva and Tantric Vows*

The Benefits of Going for Refuge

1. We become a pure Buddhist
2. We establish the foundation for taking all other vows
3. We purify the negative karma that we have accumulated in the past
4. We daily accumulate a vast amount of merit
5. We are held back from falling into the lower realms
6. We are protected from harm inflicted by humans and non-humans
7. We fulfil all our temporary and ultimate wishes
8. We quickly attain the full enlightenment of Buddhahood

Suggested reading: *Joyful Path of Good Fortune*

The Refuge Vows

1. Not to go for refuge to teachers who contradict Buddha's view, or to samsaric gods
2. To regard any image of Buddha as an actual Buddha
3. Not to harm others
4. To regard any Dharma scripture as an actual Dharma Jewel
5. Not to allow ourself to be influenced by people who reject Buddha's teaching
6. To regard anyone who wears the robes of an ordained person as an actual Sangha Jewel
7. To go for refuge to the Three Jewels again and again, remembering their good qualities and the differences between them
8. To offer the first portion of whatever we eat and drink to the Three Jewels, remembering their kindness
9. With compassion, always to encourage others to go for refuge
10. Remembering the benefits of going for refuge, to go for refuge at least three times during the day and three times during the night
11. To perform every action with complete trust in the Three Jewels
12. Never to forsake the Three Jewels even at the cost of our life, or as a joke

Suggested reading: *Joyful Path of Good Fortune* and *The New Meditation Handbook*

The Lay Pratimoksha Vows

1. To abandon killing
2. To abandon stealing
3. To abandon sexual misconduct
4. To abandon lying
5. To abandon taking intoxicants

Suggested reading: *Tantric Grounds and Paths*

The Benefits of Bodhichitta

1. We enter the gateway to the Mahayana
2. We become a Son or Daughter of the Buddhas
3. We surpass Hearers and Solitary Realizers
4. We become worthy to receive offerings and prostrations from humans and gods
5. We easily accumulate a vast amount of merit
6. We quickly destroy powerful negativities
7. We fulfil all our wishes
8. We are free from harm by spirits and so forth
9. We accomplish all the spiritual grounds and paths
10. We have a state of mind that is the source of peace and happiness for all beings

Suggested reading: *Joyful Path of Good Fortune*

The Precepts of Aspiring Bodhichitta

1. To remember the benefits of bodhichitta six times a day
2. To generate bodhichitta six times a day
3. Not to abandon any living being
4. To accumulate merit and wisdom
5. Not to cheat or deceive our Preceptors or Spiritual Guides
6. Not to criticize those who have entered the Mahayana
7. Not to cause others to regret their virtuous actions
8. Not to pretend to have good qualities or hide our faults without a special, pure intention

Suggested reading: *The New Eight Steps to Happiness*

The Root Downfalls of the Bodhisattva Vows

1. Praising ourself and scorning others
2. Not giving wealth or Dharma
3. Not accepting others' apologies
4. Abandoning the Mahayana
5. Stealing the property of the Three Jewels
6. Abandoning Dharma
7. Taking away saffron robes
8. Committing the five heinous actions
9. Holding wrong views
10. Destroying places such as towns
11. Explaining emptiness to those who are likely to misunderstand
12. Causing others to abandon the Mahayana
13. Causing others to abandon the Pratimoksha
14. Belittling the Hinayana
15. Speaking falsely about profound emptiness
16. Accepting property that has been stolen from the Three Jewels
17. Making bad rules
18. Giving up bodhichitta

Suggested reading: *The Bodhisattva Vow*

The Secondary Downfalls of the Bodhisattva Vows

Downfalls that obstruct the perfection of giving

1. Not making offerings to the Three Jewels every day
2. Indulging in worldly pleasures out of attachment
3. Being disrespectful to those who received the Bodhisattva vows before us
4. Not replying to others
5. Not accepting invitations
6. Not accepting gifts
7. Not giving Dharma to those who desire it

Downfalls that obstruct the perfection of moral discipline

8. Forsaking those who have broken their moral discipline
9. Not acting in ways that cause others to generate faith
10. Doing little to benefit others
11. Not believing that Bodhisattvas' compassion ensures that all their actions are pure
12. Acquiring wealth or fame through wrong livelihood
13. Indulging in frivolity

14. Claiming that Bodhisattvas need not abandon samsara
15. Not avoiding a bad reputation
16. Not helping others to avoid negativity

Downfalls that obstruct the perfection of patience

17. Retaliating to harm or abuse
18. Not apologizing when we have the opportunity
19. Not accepting others' apologies
20. Making no effort to control our anger

Downfalls that obstruct the perfection of effort

21. Gathering a circle of followers out of desire for profit or respect
22. Not trying to overcome laziness
23. Indulging in senseless conversation out of attachment

Downfalls that obstruct the perfection of mental stabilization

24. Neglecting to train in mental stabilization
25. Not overcoming obstacles to mental stabilization
26. Being preoccupied with the taste of mental stabilization

Downfalls that obstruct the perfection of wisdom

27. Abandoning the Hinayana
28. Studying the Hinayana to the detriment of our Mahayana practice
29. Studying non-Dharma subjects without a good reason
30. Becoming engrossed in non-Dharma subjects for their own sake
31. Criticizing other Mahayana traditions
32. Praising ourself and scorning others
33. Making no effort to study Dharma
34. Preferring to rely upon books rather than upon our Spiritual Guide

Downfalls that obstruct the moral discipline of benefiting others

35. Not going to the assistance of those in need
36. Neglecting to take care of the sick
37. Not acting to dispel suffering
38. Not helping others to overcome their bad habits
39. Not returning help to those who benefit us
40. Not relieving the distress of others
41. Not giving to those who seek charity
42. Not taking special care of disciples
43. Not acting in accordance with the inclinations of others
44. Not praising the good qualities of others
45. Not doing wrathful actions when appropriate
46. Not using miracle powers, threatening actions, and so forth

Suggested reading: *The Bodhisattva Vow*

The Commitments of Training the Mind

1. Do not allow your practice of training the mind to cause inappropriate behaviour
2. Do not allow your practice of training the mind to contradict your vows
3. Do not practise training the mind with partiality
4. Remain natural while changing your aspiration
5. Do not speak about degenerated limbs
6. Never think about others' faults
7. Purify your greatest delusion first
8. Abandon any hope for results
9. Abandon poisonous food
10. Do not follow delusions
11. Do not retaliate to verbal abuse
12. Do not wait in ambush
13. Do not offend others
14. Do not transfer your own faults or burdens onto others
15. Do not misuse Dharma
16. Do not aim at being the first to get the best
17. Do not turn a god into a demon
18. Do not seek happiness by causing unhappiness to others

Suggested reading: *Universal Compassion*

The Precepts of Training the Mind

1. Do all yogas by one
2. Perform every suppression of interference by one
3. There are two activities: one at the beginning and one at the end
4. Endure both, whichever arises
5. Guard both as you would your life
6. Train in the three difficulties
7. Practise the three main causes
8. Become acquainted with the three non-degenerations
9. Possess the three inseparables
10. Train without bias towards the objects
11. It is important to train deeply and encompass all
12. Always meditate on special cases
13. Do not rely upon other conditions
14. Apply the principal practice at this time
15. Do not misinterpret
16. Do not be erratic
17. Train with certainty
18. Be released by two: investigation and analysis
19. Do not be boastful
20. Do not get angry
21. Do not be unstable
22. Do not wish for gratitude

Suggested reading: *Universal Compassion*

The Nineteen Commitments of the Five Buddha Families

The six commitments of the family of Buddha Vairochana

1. To go for refuge to Buddha
2. To go for refuge to Dharma
3. To go for refuge to Sangha
4. To refrain from non-virtue
5. To practise virtue
6. To benefit others

The four commitments of the family of Buddha Akshobya

1. To keep a vajra to remind us to emphasize the development of great bliss through meditation on the central channel
2. To keep a bell to remind us to emphasize meditation on emptiness
3. To generate ourself as the Deity while realizing all things that we normally see do not exist
4. To rely sincerely upon our Spiritual Guide who leads us to the practice of the pure moral discipline of the Pratimoksha, Bodhisattva and Tantric vows

*The four commitments of the family of
    Buddha Ratnasambhava*

1. To give material help
2. To give Dharma
3. To give fearlessness
4. To give love

*The three commitments of the family of
    Buddha Amitabha*

1. To rely upon the teachings of Sutra
2. To rely upon the teachings of the two lower classes of Tantra
3. To rely upon the teachings of the two higher classes of Tantra

*The two commitments of the family of
    Buddha Amoghasiddhi*

1. To make offerings to our Spiritual Guide
2. To strive to maintain purely all the vows we have taken

Suggested reading: *Tantric Grounds and Paths*

The Fourteen Root Downfalls of the Secret Mantra Vows

1. Abusing or scorning our Spiritual Guide
2. Showing contempt for the precepts
3. Criticizing our vajra brothers and sisters
4. Abandoning love for any being
5. Giving up aspiring or engaging bodhichitta
6. Scorning the Dharma of Sutra or Tantra
7. Revealing secrets to an unsuitable person
8. Abusing our body
9. Abandoning emptiness
10. Relying upon malevolent friends
11. Not recollecting the view of emptiness
12. Destroying others' faith
13. Not maintaining commitment objects
14. Scorning women

Suggested reading: *Tantric Grounds and Paths*

The Branch Commitments

The commitments of abandonment are

to abandon negative actions, especially killing, stealing, sexual misconduct, lying and taking intoxicants

The commitments of reliance are

to rely sincerely upon our Spiritual Guide, to be respectful towards our vajra brothers and sisters, and to observe the ten virtuous actions

The additional commitments of abandonment are

to abandon the causes of turning away from the Mahayana, to avoid scorning gods and to avoid stepping over sacred objects

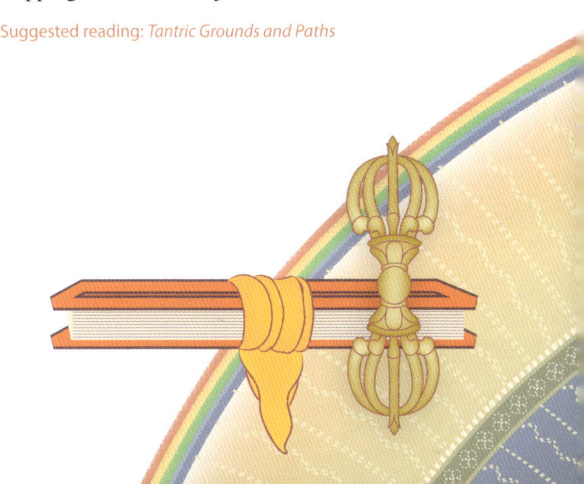

Suggested reading: *Tantric Grounds and Paths*

The Gross Downfalls of the Secret Mantra Vows

1. Relying upon an unqualified mudra
2. Engaging in union without the three recognitions
3. Showing secret substances to an unsuitable person
4. Fighting or arguing during a tsog offering ceremony
5. Giving false answers to questions asked out of faith
6. Staying seven days in the home of someone who rejects the Vajrayana
7. Pretending to be a Yogi while remaining imperfect
8. Revealing holy Dharma to those with no faith
9. Engaging in mandala actions without completing a close retreat
10. Needlessly transgressing the Pratimoksha or Bodhisattva precepts
11. Acting in contradiction to the *Fifty Verses on the Spiritual Guide*

Suggested reading: *Tantric Grounds and Paths*

The Uncommon Commitments of Mother Tantra

1. To perform all physical actions first with our left, to make offerings to our Spiritual Guide, and never to abuse him
2. To abandon union with those unqualified
3. While in union, not to be separated from the view of emptiness
4. Never to lose appreciation for the path of attachment
5. Never to forsake the two kinds of mudra
6. To strive mainly for the external and internal methods
7. Never to release seminal fluid; to rely upon pure behaviour
8. To abandon repulsion when tasting bodhichitta

Suggested reading: *Tantric Grounds and Paths*

*Dedicated to the long life and perfect health of
Venerable Geshe Kelsang Gyatso Rinpoche*

This booklet is published under the auspices of the
NKT-IKBU International Temples Project Fund
and the profit from its sale is designated for
public benefit through this fund.
Reg. Charity number 1015054 (England)
Find out more: www.tharpa.com/benefit-all-world-peace

Colophon: Extracted from the following books *The Bodhisattva Vow, Joyful Path of Good Fortune, The New Eight Steps to Happiness, The New Meditation Handbook, Tantric Grounds and Paths* and *Universal Compassion*. More detail on all the vows and commitments can be found in these and the other suggested books, which are available from Tharpa Publications:

tharpa.com